On the afternoon of 1 March 1912, [illegible]s West End looked the same as [illegible] women walked past the big shop[illegible]ndows. Suddenly, everything chan[illegible] the women took hammers from their muffs and started to smash the shop windows.

This is what Oxford Street in London's West End looked like in 1912.

Who were all these women, and why did they smash the windows?

They were called the 'suffragettes', and they were angry because at that time, women could not vote. Only men could vote and help to choose the Government. The suffragettes wanted votes for women.

The Houses of Parliament in London. The suffragettes wanted to be able to vote for members of Parliament.

Their leader was Emmeline Pankhurst. She said the suffragettes must act violently to make people listen to them. Emmeline Pankhurst became the most famous suffragette of all.

Emmeline Pankhurst

Emmeline was born in Manchester in 1858. When she was twenty-one years old she married Richard Pankhurst.

Over the next six years Emmeline and Richard had four children, three girls and a boy. At first Emmeline was too busy looking after her children to help other women.

Richard Pankhurst

Emmeline and Richard had three daughters – Sylvia, Adela and Christabel – and one son.

When Emmeline was thirty, she began her work for women again. She helped some girls who made matches in east London. The girls were badly paid for a very unhealthy job. When one girl was sacked, the rest went on strike. Emmeline Pankhurst helped them to fight for more money. The match-girl who was sacked was given her job back.

Some of the match makers who went on strike

Emmeline Pankhurst also visited a workhouse near her home in Manchester. People who had no home or no job had to live in the workhouse. They were often cold and hungry there. Emmeline helped to get better clothes and food for them, and to make the workhouse a better place to live in.

Women eating a meal in a workhouse

When Emmeline's husband Richard died, she went to work in the slums of Manchester, where poor people lived. She saw how hard their life was. She decided there was only one way to change things for the better – and that was to give women the vote.

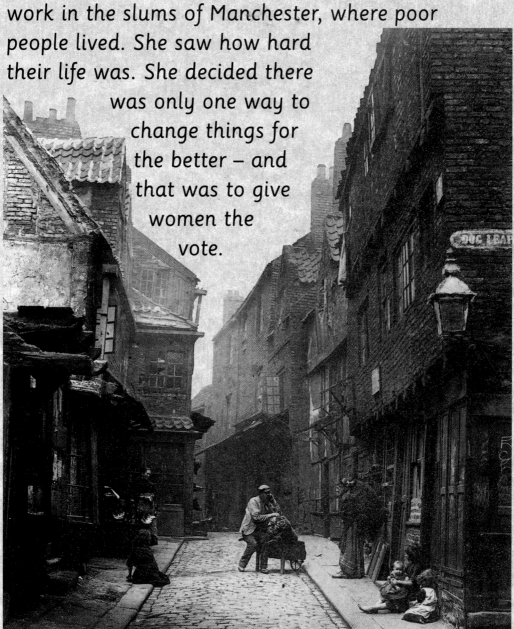

Slums in the north of England

Emmeline and her daughter Christabel led a group of women to form the Women's Social and Political Union. They wanted to fight for votes for women – and they meant fight. They were called the suffragettes, and their adventures filled the newspapers for many years.

Emmeline with Christabel (in the dark skirt) and some friends in their garden in Manchester

A suffragette is arrested outside Buckingham Palace in London.

In 1906, Britain had a new government. The suffragettes hoped it would pass a law giving the vote to women, but it did not. So they decided to fight harder. Many women were arrested.

The suffragettes fought with police outside
Parliament. They broke the windows of government

Emmeline Pankhurst is arrested outside Buckingham Palace
and carried away by a policeman.

offices, post offices and banks. They chained themselves to railings in Downing Street, where the Prime Minister lived, and outside Buckingham Palace. They set fire to post boxes and government buildings. Emmeline Pankhurst and her friends were arrested and told to pay a fine. They refused to pay, so they were sent to prison. In prison, they went on 'hunger strike', and refused to eat. They were ready to starve to death for what they believed in.

Emmeline and her daughter Christabel in their prison clothes

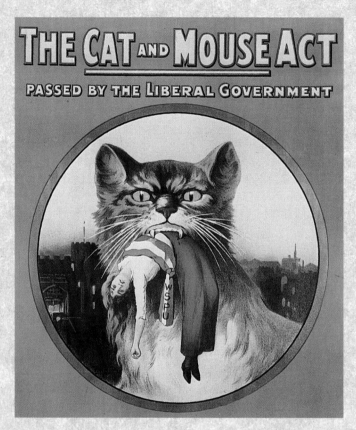

THE CAT AND MOUSE ACT
PASSED BY THE LIBERAL GOVERNMENT

WSPU

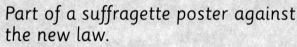

Part of a suffragette poster against the new law.

Then the government passed a new law. It said hunger-strikers could be freed from prison when they became weak. Then, when they were better, they were arrested again. The law was called 'the Cat and Mouse Act' because it reminded people of the way a cat plays with a mouse. Emmeline Pankhurst was set free and arrested again eight times.

Emily Davidson stops the Derby, and dies.

Emily's funeral

In June 1913 there was a new horror story in the newspapers. The Derby, Britain's most famous horse race, had to stop when a suffragette, called Emily Davidson, ran on to the track in front of the King's horse. She was killed. Thousands of people watched her funeral.

The suffragettes' battle went on. Once they tried to march to Buckingham Palace but police stopped them. But one young suffragette did get inside the Palace. She asked Queen Mary to 'stop torturing women.'

Queen Mary said suffragettes were undignified and tiresome!

But in 1914 a more important story filled the newspapers. On 4 August 1914 Germany and Britain declared war, and four years of terrible fighting began.

Emmeline Pankhurst made speeches to persuade men to join the army and navy. Votes for women had to wait until the war was over.

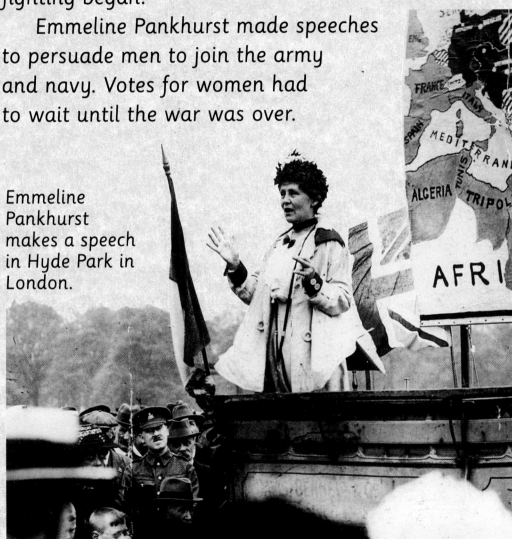

Emmeline Pankhurst makes a speech in Hyde Park in London.

Women worked hard at home while their men were away fighting. The government said their hard work was important to Britain. When the war ended, in 1918, women over thirty were given the vote. Ten years later the voting age for women became the same as for men – twenty-one. In the same year, Emmeline Pankhurst died. She had lived just long enough to see her hopes come true.

Today, in Britain, all men and women can vote when they are eighteen.

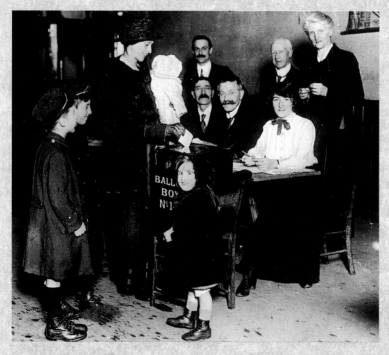

In 1918 women voted for the first time.

Important dates

1858 Emmeline Goulden was born
1879 Emmeline married Richard Pankhurst
1880 First daughter Christabel was born
1898 Husband Richard died
1903 Women's Social and Political Union (WSPU) formed
1906 First suffragette march, to the Houses of Parliament
1909 A suffragette goes on hunger strike for the first time
1913 Cat and Mouse Act passed
Emily Davidson died after stopping the Derby
1914 World War I began
1917 Emmeline went to Canada
1918 World War I ended
Women over thirty given the vote
1928 Women over twenty-one given the vote
Emmeline Pankhurst died

A suffragette medal with a photograph of Emmeline Pankhurst

Keywords

Parliament
members of Parliament pass laws and help to govern the country

suffragette
women who fought for votes for women

to vote
to choose (members of Parliament)

Index